Pathways to Co-operation

Starting Points for Co-operative Learning

Dot Walker & Pamela Brown

ELEANOR CURTAIN
PUBLISHING

First published in 1994
ELEANOR CURTAIN PUBLISHING
906 Malvern Road
Armadale 3143
Australia

Copyright © 1994 Dot Walker and Pamela Brown

All rights reserved. No part of this publication may be reproduced in any form without prior permission from the publisher. This does not apply to Figure 2.1 on page 13, which may be reproduced by the purchaser for individual and classroom use only.

National Library of Australia
Cataloguing-in publication data:

Walker, Dorothy Ann, 1946–
Pathways to co-operation: starting points for co-operative learning.
Bibliography.
ISBN 1 875327 20 7.

1. Group work in education. 2. Team learning approach in education. 3. Primary school teaching. I. Brown, Pamela Grace, 1939–   . II. Title.

372.1395

Production by Sylvana Scannapiego, Island Graphics
Edited by Deborah Doyle (Living Proof – Book Editing)
Cover and text design by David Constable
Cover photograph by Sara Curtain
Typeset in 13/15 pt Baskerville
by EMS Typesetting, South Melbourne
Printed in Australia by Impact Printing

Distributed in North America by:
Peguis Publishers
100-318 McDermot Avenue
Winnipeg, MB
Canada R3A 0A2

CONTENTS

FOREWORD

Across Australia and in other parts of the world, teachers are increasingly acknowledging that co-operation is essential if our world is to survive in the future. They agree that working together, collaboratively, benefits children's learning as well as their own, and they understand that in a true learning community, co-operation is embedded in the very fabric of classroom life.

Although these important principles have been agreed on, it remains that in co-operative-learning workshops the question most often asked is 'How do we get started?' This is not an easy question to answer, because co-operative learning is neither a 'program' nor a pre-packaged set of steps: in journeying towards creating a co-operative classroom we may take many pathways, and the journey may be different for each of us.

What we need are starting points that offer a multiplicity of possibilities that are practical but that at the same time encourage us to reflect on our beliefs and current practices. Dot and Pam have written *Pathways to Co-operation* for this purpose. The book reflects both their wealth of classroom experience and their expertise as consultants.

Pathways to Co-operation will be of great benefit to teachers for whom co-operative learning is a brand-new challenge. Teachers who are experienced in the field of co-operative learning will also find it useful, as a way of expanding on and reflecting their repertoire of practical strategies.

All in all, *Pathways to Co-operation* is a rich and practical resource and is a most welcome addition to the field of co-operative learning.

Joan Dalton

Joan Dalton
President
Australasian Association for Co-operative Education

INTRODUCTION

In our work as effective-learning and teaching advisers, we have found that one of the greatest challenges for teachers is to put theory into practice successfully. The essence of this challenge lies in the fact that every school, every class, and each individual child, may require various approaches if theory is to be implemented effectively. Another factor that contributes to the challenge is that we, as teachers, bring various stages of – and types of – experience, as well as our preferred approaches, to every learning–teaching situation.

Many excellent books have been written about co-operative learning, and some of them are referred to throughout this book. We nevertheless believe that, as teachers, we can benefit from using multiple opportunities to consider the basic philosophy and strategies that underpin co-operative learning and teaching. In the book we have called these multiple opportunities 'pathways to co-operation'. The eight 'pathways' provide choices for us to make during our journeying towards co-operative learning.

In writing the book, our purpose is to acknowledge current theory and to put together practical, theoretically sound strategies that can help teachers in making their responses to the many demands inherent in their work. The strategies have been useful to us and our colleagues in planning for, and facilitating, effective learning and teaching. Although we have used specific strategies in each pathway, the strategies can have multiple uses across pathways.

In choosing pathways and strategies, teachers can readily design programs to meet children's individual learning requirements. The potential to involve more children in active learning, both now and in the future, has definitely been established in our approaches. The mere 'giving of information' has long been considered inadequate for the satisfactory cognitive, psychological and physical development of humans – child or adult. Now, as well as for the future, we need ways through which we can encourage children to be independent and interdependent learners. These ways must include emphasising an interactive balance between 'how' we learn and 'what' we learn, and the pathways suggest considered ideas for bringing this about.

The book's format is intended to encourage teachers to adapt and own the ideas and strategies contained in it. It should be considered a flexible journal that teachers use for planning, reflecting, recording tried strategies and outcomes, and adding ideas and achievements.

When using the book, teachers will naturally be drawn into a process that culminates in co-operative learning. The book supports their efforts by including the following four 'guideposts' for each pathway.

- Prerequisite understandings and beliefs
- Effective teaching strategies for implementing each pathway in the classroom
- Real-life examples of the pathway in practice
- Ideas for the effective strategies for classroom implementation

The material is appropriate for a wide range of children's age and ability. By using the book as a personal journal, teachers can build on their knowledge of the processes required in order to help children create their own futures.

We hope each pathway provides a starting point and a framework through which teachers can enjoy being reflective practitioners – creators and implementors of dynamic theory.

ACKNOWLEDGEMENTS

A moving circle of children and adults influenced us when we were writing the book: the scholars and writers Jim Butler, Stephen Covey and Joan Dalton; also our colleagues in most recent years, creative practitioners Louise Constance, Lorne Mourilyan, Vicki Russcoe, Patricia Paten and Nikki Dredge, who have, knowingly or unknowingly, been part of our consciousness in creating the 'pathways' – we are grateful for being able to connect with their wisdoms and creative practices. Susan Clark did a 'top job' typing the manuscript, and Kym Graafland helped when time was short. Finally, in thanking each other, we complete a circle of co-operation, of which this book is one outcome.

PART ONE

The eight pathways to co-operation

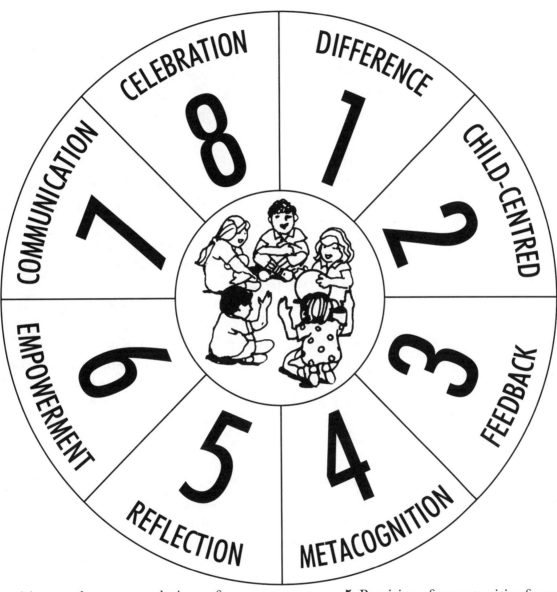

1 Recognition and accommodation of *difference*

2 Design and implementation of *child-centred* programs

3 Provision of constructive *feedback* to the individual child and groups of children

4 Acknowledgement that *metacognition* is an optimum level for thinking and learning

5 Provision of opportunities for *reflection*

6 *Empowerment* of children as learners

7 Acknowledgement of the critical nature of quality *communication*

8 Acknowledgement of the importance of *celebration* in learning

GETTING THE MOST OUT OF THIS BOOK

The eight pathways to co-operation can be used in various ways by individual teachers, groups of teachers or the whole school.

The book's format is designed in a way that encourages teachers to make it their own. When using it as a journal for planning and reflection, teachers can benefit by adding their own ideas, strategies and references.

Following are nine suggestions for individual and collegial use of the book.

SUGGESTIONS

1 Individual teachers could clarify their own beliefs about learning and identify to what extent these beliefs are being put into practice.

2 As a group of staff members or an interest group, teachers could brainstorm ideas for effective strategies that relate to a specific pathway.

3 The whole school could focus on and develop a particular pathway over the period of a term or a school year.

4 Groups of teachers within a school could focus on and develop various pathways and then share the outcomes.

5 Professional associations could focus on and develop particular pathways.

6 Groups of teachers or whole schools could use all the pathways to support curriculum development.

7 The pathways could be used as discussion starters.

8 The pathways could be used with parents in order to build their understanding of effective learning and teaching.

9 Children could be involved in creating activities for some of the pathways, for example the last one, 'Acknowledgement of the importance of celebration in learning'.

1 DIFFERENCE

Recognition and accommodation of difference

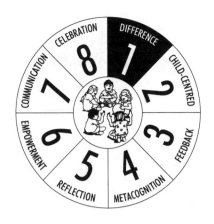

GUIDEPOSTS

PREREQUISITE UNDERSTANDINGS AND BELIEFS

As a teacher, do you
- believe that difference is a positive factor that can inspire creative-teaching strategies?
- recognise that differences expressed through culture and attitude are socially constructed?
- acknowledge that unwarranted assumptions may be made about physical and social differences?

EFFECTIVE STRATEGIES FOR CLASSROOM IMPLEMENTATION

- Build a positive classroom climate.

- Build and maintain a feeling of worth as an integral component of your total program.

- Model the acceptance and valuing of difference.

- Plan and design for co-operative-learning opportunities.

- Create opportunities for the community of learners to recognise and celebrate the individual differences within the group.

It was almost Christmas time and the children in Maria's Year 2–3 class had asked to make Christmas cards for their families. Maria gathered the children together and they looked at some commercially produced cards – how they were set out and what types of greetings had to be included. The children were just about to embark on making their own cards when Ishia said, quietly, 'Excuse me, miss, but I'm not allowed to do this; my family doesn't believe in Christmas.'

Before Maria could respond, Lee, in a very loud voice, exploded, 'How could anyone not believe in Christmas? – that's dumb.'

Maria, in a very calm voice and placing one hand on Lee's shoulder, addressed the whole class: 'Remember, way back at the beginning of the year, we did lots of work looking at how different we all were. Some of us had different skin and different noses and different knees and toes, and we decided that's okay.'

The children all nodded, remembering. 'Well,' continued Maria, 'some of us believe in different things as well.'

'Like who'll win the Winfield Cup, miss?' asked Tim.

'Yes, sort of, Tim. Everyone has a right to believe in what he or she thinks is right. Okay: can anyone give Ishia an idea for a different card she could make?'

'She could make a "happy" card,' suggested Steven. 'It doesn't have to be "Happy Christmas" – it could just be wishing someone a happy day.'

'What a great idea, Steven!' responded Maria. 'Do you think that would be okay, Ishia?'

'Yes, I like that,' said Ishia, smiling.

'Can I make a "happy" card too?' asked Lee.

'And me?' asked Tim.

'And me?' asked Jan.

'Of course,' said Maria. 'You may choose what type of card you would like to make, and you can work on your own or with a partner or with your home group. I'll give you two minutes to discuss quietly, with others, how you might like to make your cards.'

The children turned to each other and started discussing their cards.

IDEAS FOR EFFECTIVE STRATEGIES

 'SUPERSTARS' BOOK

Make up a class 'superstars' book to include everyone's photograph and talents.

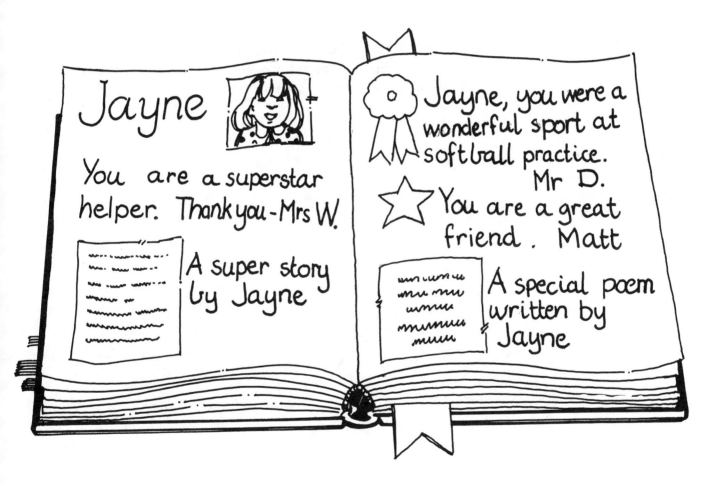

 'SECRET FRIENDS'

Place each child's name – and the teacher's – on a small slip of paper and put all the pieces in a container. Ask each child to pull a name out of the container – that person will be the child's 'secret friend' for the day. If a child pulls out his or her own name, ask him or her to replace the slip and choose another one.

During the day, make it each child's responsibility to help his or her secret friend in any way possible. At the end of the day, sit the children and teacher in a 'sharing' circle and share information about who they think was their secret friend and why.

Walker and Ferencz (1982) suggest using whole-class reflection on what it felt like when a secret friend was helping you.

 USE OF PHOTOGRAPHS

Mount the class members' photographs – and the teacher's – on the door to the classroom.

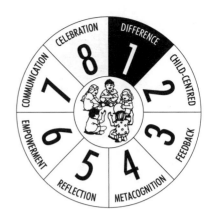

 **'CIRCLE' GAMES**

Susan Hill (1992) suggests to sit the whole class, including the teacher, in a circle. Let each child turn to the person on his or her right and, using a predetermined phrase, say, 'I'm glad you're you because …'

Other alternatives could be as follows.

- 'You make me happy when you …'
- 'I'm glad you're in our group because …'
- 'I like it best when you …'

It is important to remember that in any activity such as this, the 'pass' option is available to everyone.

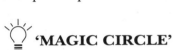 **'MAGIC CIRCLE'**

Begin slowly.

Involve children in setting the rules or expectations for 'magic circle'. According to 'Primary Focus', a (1989) video produced by the Tasmanian Education Department's Curriculum Branch, the two most important of these are that

- what is said in the circle stays in the circle, and
- everyone gets a turn.

These expectations must be reinforced before each session commences.

Three good starting points are

- 'I'm glad I'm me because I can …' for the first session,
- 'I'm glad I'm me because I feel …' for the second session, and
- 'I'm glad you're you because you …' for the third session. (Each child addresses the person on his or her right.)

It is important that the teacher use incidents or situations that may have arisen during the week.

For particular groups of children, you might wish to repeat these first three sessions until you feel that the class has accepted the structure of 'magic circle' and that trust has been built up.

The 'pass' option is always there for children who do not wish to actively participate. Although some children may continue to use the 'pass' option, they should remain in the circle, because that way they will still be exposed to the other children's modelling.

Once children are confident with the 'magic circle' procedure, it is up to the teacher to introduce suitable topics. Some ideas are listed as follows.

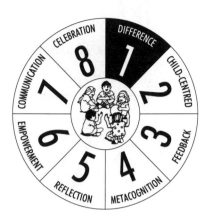

- Friendship
- Pride
- Anger
- Happiness
- Joy
- Fear
- Forgiveness
- Jealousy
- Love
- Success

The first time around the circle, each child shares what makes him or her feel that particular emotion.

The second time around, the children share what that particular emotion feels like for them.

The session can be concluded by holding a 'question time' session, if the group has established trust.

2 CHILD-CENTRED

Design and implementation of child-centred programs

GUIDEPOSTS

PREREQUISITE UNDERSTANDINGS AND BELIEFS

As a teacher, do you

- believe that children develop cognitively, socially, emotionally and physically at their own rate?
- accept that each child brings to the learning experience a rich and varied background of prior knowledge?
- acknowledge that learning experiences are most effective when they can be linked to prior knowledge, are relevant to the learner, and are developmentally appropriate?
- believe that differences can be creative?

EFFECTIVE STRATEGIES FOR CLASSROOM IMPLEMENTATION

- Listen, observe, monitor and reflect in order to create your base for planning.

- Focus on the understanding of concepts.

- Provide opportunities to develop skills as a means to achieving the understanding of concepts.

- Use relevant content and contexts in order to ensure that transference of learning takes place.

- Consistently provide opportunities to celebrate learning and learners.

- Value and incorporate children's ideas and suggestions within the programs.

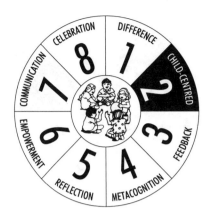

THE PATHWAY IN PRACTICE: A VIGNETTE

Sue was feeling very happy with the maths session she had prepared for her Year 1–2 class. Her main focus for the week was on counting, ordering of numbers and comparison of size.

Sue uses a 'contract' system with her class, which incorporates

- a maths learning centre that accommodates various learning styles, and
- the building of choice into her program.

On one particular day, Sue had enlisted a parent's help in working outdoors with children, using large blocks in order to address the concept of 'smallest to largest'.

Just as children were about to begin working on their contracts, Jason, a very quiet class member, suddenly addressed Sue: 'What about my digger? – you said yesterday that if I brought it today I could show it to everyone; you promised.'

'Yes, I did, Jason. Why don't you go and get it now?' replied Sue.

Jason proudly displayed the large Tonker toy to the group, and shared his wealth of knowledge about the various parts of the machine and how it worked.

The children listened and were clearly interested; several asked questions, to which Jason responded confidently.

'I wonder,' said Sue, 'whether we could use Jason's digger to carry out some of our maths activities – what do you think?'

'We could build a track for it with the blocks outside that got bigger and bigger,' suggested Damien.

'What a great idea, Damien!' responded Sue. 'Does anyone have any other ideas?'

'We could see what size block the front part of the machine can lift up,' suggested Mrs Davis, the parent helper.

'That sounds like fun!' responded Sue. 'Would you like to organise the blocks for that activity, Mrs Davis? Thank you.'

'We could count all the different moving bits,' said Sam.

'That's a good idea, too!' said Sue. 'Let's write these suggestions up on butcher's paper, and you can choose one of the activities we've come up with as part of your contract. Is it okay to use your digger as part of our maths lesson, Jason?'

'Oh, yes!' said Jason, proudly setting his toy down in the centre of the circle.

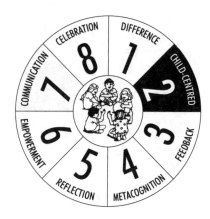

The children moved into their maths contract time, many of them choosing one of the activities centred around Jason's toy.

Sue moved around the maths groups, supporting and questioning and making notes on a small pad she always carried with her.

After the session, Sue transferred her notes to her program. In Jason's file, she made a special comment about his interest in and knowledge of large machines; she also noted a new confidence in Jason's interactions with the other children during the maths session.

Finally, she added a note to herself to discuss with the class the idea of other class members bringing along favourite toys to build into the maths program.

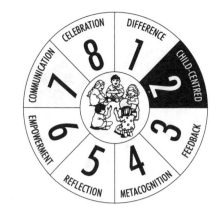

IDEAS FOR EFFECTIVE STRATEGIES

Photocopy the following diagram, which summarises the components of child-centred planning, and pin it on your personal noticeboard.

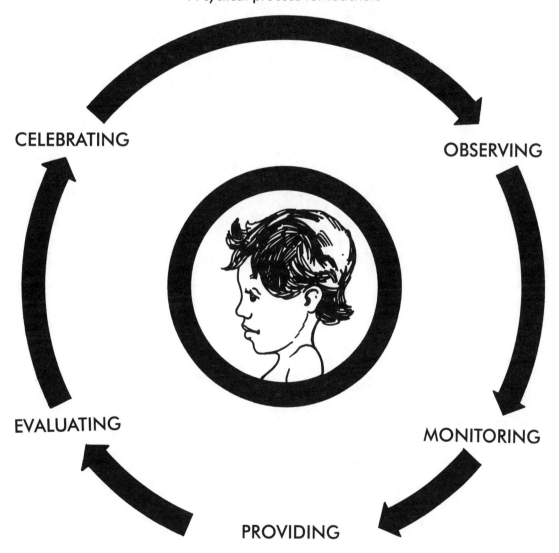

CHILD-CENTRED PLANNING
A cyclical process for teachers

CELEBRATING

OBSERVING

MONITORING

PROVIDING

EVALUATING

Figure 2.1, page 13, 'Child-centred planning' diagram.
From *Pathways to Co-operation* by Walker and Brown © Dot Walker and Pamela Brown, 1994. This page may be reproduced for classroom use.

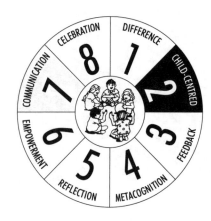

Plan activities to enable you to gain insight into children's differences, interests and preferred learning styles.

Use curriculum documents to identify key concepts to be focused on and the skills children require in order to explore these concepts.

Use child-identified topics, interests and contexts in developing these skills.

Encourage children to use a variety of ways for expressing their understanding of the concepts, for example mime, writing, and audio or video tapes.

Hold class meetings. (See the 'Communication' pathway, page 52.)

Play the 'magic circle' game. (See the 'Difference' pathway, page 7.)

Maintain portfolios on individual children, as follows.

PORTFOLIOS: THE DYNAMIC BASE FOR CHILD-CENTRED PLANNING

Maintaining a portfolio is one way to build up a holistic and ongoing picture of a child. It is important that teachers understand why portfolios are required and when materials should be included in them.

WHY?
- To monitor children's development
- To provide a holistic view of a child
- To give parents, administrators and other support personnel an up-to-date profile on individual children
- To display teachers' accountability

WHEN?
- When a child has mastered a competency
- When concern exists about some aspect of a child's development or behaviour
- When changes are taking place in a child's attitudes, processes, skills or knowledge

Portfolios should be shared with other teachers, administrators, parents and children. Once a decision has been made to use portfolios, teachers will find them an invaluable tool in designing developmentally appropriate programs.

The following table sets out the methods of tracking development that can be included in a portfolio.

METHODS OF TRACKING DEVELOPMENT THAT CAN BE INCLUDED IN A PORTFOLIO

Method	What?	How?
Observation	• Checklists • Journals • Anecdotal records • Notes • Video or audio tapes	• Use a variety of observation methods that suit your teaching style. • Make use of other teachers, aides and support staff. • Date all observations.
Work samples	• Include samples from all curriculum areas. • Reading logs • Artwork • Photocopies from workbooks • Samples of writing • Photographs of models or construction projects	• Some samples may require an explanation to be attached about why they have been included. • Date all samples. • Encourage children to suggest work samples for inclusion in portfolios.
Students' self-assessment and peer assessment	• Learning logs • 'Sharing' circles • Personal spelling • Feedback from group work on how the groups worked together	• Provide feedback sheets or reflection time following co-operative-learning sessions. • Encourage children to review their portfolios and write comments. • Pair-share the portfolios with teacher or child.

A sample of the material that could be included in a Year 5 student's portfolio

WHO?

Name: John Brown
Age: 10 years
Year level: 5

WHAT?

A photograph of a scale model of a Tyrannosaurus Rex (dinosaur) that he and four other children built over a three-week period

SAMPLE OF TEACHER'S WRITTEN OBSERVATIONS ATTACHED TO THE PHOTOGRAPH:

'14 April   This is the first time this year that John has worked consistently with a group of children in order to achieve a common goal.'

'30 April   The dinosaur project has been completed and John has worked extremely well with the group. I have asked him to write a personal reflection for his portfolio, about how he felt during and after the project.'

JOHN'S PERSONAL REFLECTION:

'1 May   I really liked working on the Tyrannosaurus Rex project. We all helped with different bits. When it was finished we showed it to other classes. I felt really proud when people said it was good.'

FEEDBACK SHEET

The following 'self-assessment record sheet' could be included in John's portfolio and in the portfolios of some of the other children involved in the group.

SELF-ASSESSMENT RECORD SHEET

YOUR NAME: _____

GROUP'S NAME: _____

TOPIC: _____

Name three things that helped you solve this challenge or investigation.

1 _____

2 _____

3 _____

I/we were good at

_____

_____

I/we could improve by

_____

_____

_____

3 FEEDBACK

Provision of constructive feedback to the individual child and groups of children

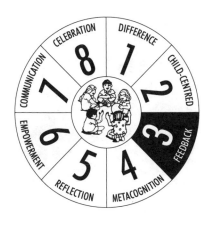

GUIDEPOSTS

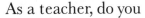

PREREQUISITE UNDERSTANDINGS AND BELIEFS

As a teacher, do you
- believe that all children develop at their own rates?
- acknowledge the value of giving the learner specific feedback?
- accept the efficacy of co-operative learning and therefore feedback for groups?
- have knowledge and understanding of the developmental signposts in children's cognitive, physical, social and emotional growth?

EFFECTIVE STRATEGIES FOR CLASSROOM IMPLEMENTATION

○ Focus on observing and on giving feedback to two or three children each day.

○ Make provision, within your program, to record children's development in relation to developmental signposts.

○ Be an active listener, and provide children with feedback.

○ Develop encouraging, inviting language that turns 'negatives' into 'positives'.

○ Make time, within your program, for both children and teacher to practise reflection.

○ Consistently model positive feedback.

○ Provide opportunities for constructive peer feedback as well as teacher feedback.

Leonie was sitting in a circle with her twenty-six Year 6–7 students. 'Well, we're almost finished the science unit on 'air'. How do you think it went?'

Each student had placed in front of him or her a small card with his or her name on it. Several students turned their cards over, indicating they would like to answer the question or share an idea or thought.

'Jenny, what would you like to share?' asked Leonie.

'I really enjoyed the experiments with the balloons – they were fun, but the one where we had to measure air pressure with the bicycle pump was really hard,' replied Jenny.

'Yes,' responded Leonie, glancing at the book in front of her, 'I've got written here in my learning log that if we did this unit again I'd use a new bicycle pump. Nick, what would you like to say?'

'Mark and I, we liked working at the learning centre, and we thought up two challenges for the others to try,' replied Nick.

'Yes,' responded Leonie, 'that challenge you two thought up with the candle flame in the jar was really successful. It made everyone who tried it think about what was happening to the air in the jar. Meg, what would you like to say?'

This sharing continued for another ten minutes and included opportunities for all the class members to be involved and have their ideas acknowledged.

Leonie then went on, 'Okay, turn to the person next to you, and you have five minutes to agree on the three most interesting things you've learnt about air during this unit.'

After five minutes Leonie explained, 'Our job now is to join with another pair and, as a group, decide on just two of the most interesting things about air, and those two things will go into our Year 6–7 'science book of amazing facts'.

IDEAS FOR EFFECTIVE STRATEGIES

Keep broadly based developmental portfolios on each child. (See the 'portfolios' idea in the 'Child-centred' pathway, page 15.)

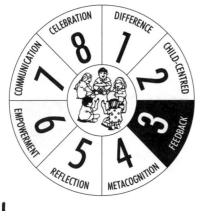

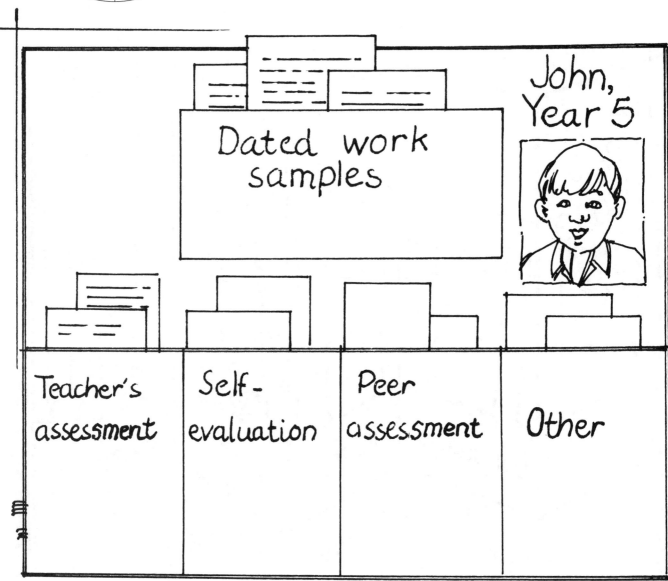

Dated work samples

John, Year 5

Teacher's assessment	Self-evaluation	Peer assessment	Other

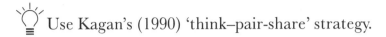 Make use of video and/or audiotaping for both children and teachers.

Use Kagan's (1990) 'think–pair-share' strategy.

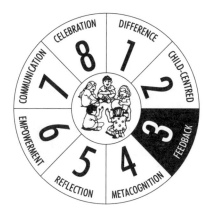

Make time for whole-class reflection and feedback from the class circle.

Maintain individual and/or class learning logs.

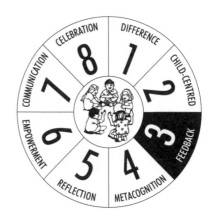

Today I had trouble with long multiplication, but Mrs M. sat down with me and Allan and showed us how to do it. I still didn't get it, so Allan and I worked on one together. We used the blocks, and then I could do it. Mrs M. made a big deal out of it, and I had to go and show Mrs R. Her class gave me a big clap. I like my multiplication now.

4 METACOGNITION

Acknowledgement that metacognition is an optimum level for thinking and learning

GUIDEPOSTS

PREREQUISITE UNDERSTANDINGS AND BELIEFS

As a teacher, do you
- understand that metacognition is knowing the thinking strategies we use in order to gain knowledge and understandings?
- accept that metacognitive awareness promotes and enriches learning?
- agree that all children, in their learning, can benefit from using metacognitive processes regardless of age or abilities?
- agree that understanding how 'I' learn helps my understanding of how others may learn?

EFFECTIVE STRATEGIES FOR CLASSROOM IMPLEMENTATION

○ Plan programs that provide children with opportunities to become aware of their own thinking.

○ Question children in an open-ended way about the learning processes they use.

○ Use Bloom's *Taxonomy* as a framework for making children aware of various ways of thinking.

○ Use the various forms of reflection – oral, written and cognitive – with individuals and/or groups.

○ Model metacognitive processes for children.

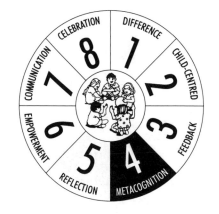

THE PATHWAY IN PRACTICE: TWO VIGNETTES

Metacognitive awareness is developmental and should be integral in learning programs. Metacognition can be developed through

* teachers' questioning,
* children questioning their own learning–thinking processes, and
* questioning other children and adults about how they went about doing or learning something.

In teaching metacognitive awareness, we seek to develop three cognitive capacities, as follows.

1 Development of children's capacity to recognise the various thinking strategies they are using

2 Increasing the quality and number of strategies children can use

3 Development of children's capacity to choose the most appropriate and effective strategies for various tasks, problems and challenges

VIGNETTE 1

Metacognition can become explicit during everyday learning experiences. In pairs, for example, four young children had been finding out which of two baskets had more biscuits in it.

Teacher:	'James and Tina, how did you find out which basket had more?'
James and Tina:	'We matched one from each basket until we couldn't make any more partners. (*Listing, matching*)
Teacher:	'Tim and Ian, how did you work it out?'
Tim and Ian:	'We kept giving each other one each until one basket was empty; then we knew the other basket had more.' (*Listing, pairing*)

In their thinking, both pairs of children used listing and pairing strategies in order to find out which basket held more biscuits than the other, and the teacher gave the children the labels for these strategies.

VIGNETTE 2
Various adaptations of the following types of activity are useful in helping children become aware of the thinking strategies they use. The children should be in groups of no more than five members each.

Teacher:	'Quickly write down a TV program you watched last night. In your groups, talk about what type of thinking you used to answer the question.'

Some responses from the children were

- 'I just knew it,',
- 'I remembered it,', and
- 'I put a picture in my head of me watching TV.'

Teacher:	'So the type of thinking we used was straightforward recall – we recalled facts: the knowledge that we watched " _____ " on the TV last night. Now we have another job to do. In your groups, your job is to design something that is not expensive but is very good at preventing bicycle thefts.'

After the ideas and designs were shared, the groups were asked to write down the types of thinking they used in creating their designs. To bring the thinking strategies to everyone's awareness, the types of thinking used were then brainstormed by the whole class; this could be compared with the earlier 'recall' activity.

IDEAS FOR EFFECTIVE STRATEGIES

The following three activities could follow on from the previous example in Vignette 2 (page 28).

Plan an effective and profitable bus timetable to suit the needs of a small country town.

Design a game you could share with the elderly people your class perhaps visits at the senior-citizens residential park.

Write a report about an imaginary city council's refusal to approve an application to build a fun park and swimming pool on the banks of the local river.

In each task, children also have to identify the thinking strategies they have used. This cognitive awareness contributes much to both independent and co-operative learning.

IDEAS FOR QUESTIONS
• 'How did you decide?'
• 'How might we go about it?'

'THINKING' CIRCLE
The children share with the class one thing they have learnt and also how they have learnt it.

ANALYSIS OF TEXT
How did the author influence or persuade the reader?

After the problem-solving activity, the children pair-share not only the answer but how they arrived at the solution.

VIGNETTE 3

Pam's class had indicated that during lunch hour the line-ups at the tuckshop could be very frustrating, especially for younger children.

Pam asked her class members to sit with their already established 'buddy' and discuss what could be done to solve the problem. She also asked them to record how they arrived at the solution. The time limit agreed on by both Pam and the children for completion of the task was two days. Following are some of the children's responses.

• TANIA AND FAYE

'Tania and I asked a lot of kids from all different classes a questionnaire about what they thought should be done to make the tuckshop better, and we made their answers into a kind of graph. We agree with most people that there should be certain times for each class to go and buy from the tuckshop.'

• TY AND DEAN

'We counted up all the people in the school, and we thought maybe half of them would buy their lunch each day. We divided this number into sixty minutes, which means each person should take forty-five seconds to buy something. So we decided that if everyone had a numbered ticket, the sellers could call out when it was each person's turn, and it would stop people pushing in.'

• DONNA AND MIAH

'We asked Donna's mum, who works in the tuckshop, what she thought. She said that not enough mums and dads can come and help because they work, so we think the Year 7s should take turns to serve in the tuckshop.'

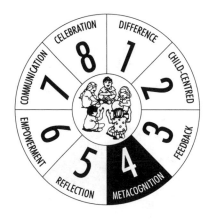

Using Bloom's *Taxonomy*, set up a learning centre around a specific unit of work. The following planning model for the emotion 'happiness' could be adapted to any age level, and other emotions could be substituted for happiness. It is only one of many ways to plan units using Bloom's *Taxonomy*.

Suggestions for other emotions that could be used, depending on the children's interests, are listed as follows.

- Fear
- Joy
- Sadness
- Greed
- Jealousy
- Excitement

FOUR POINTS ON HOW TO GET STARTED

1 Begin by brainstorming class activities and ideas using Bloom's six levels of questioning.
2 Negotiate with children
- what they know about happiness,
- what they want to find out about happiness, and
- how they will show what they have found out.
3 Plan, using all levels of Bloom's *Taxonomy*,
- whole-class activities,
- group activities, and
- individual activities.
4 Give children choice via
- contracts,
- the learning centre,
- projects, and
- daily challenges.

In all these activities, consideration has to be given to the openendedness of tasks.

• IDEAS FOR A 'HAPPINESS' PLANNING MODEL

1 KNOWLEDGE

Make a list of 'happy' words.

Make a list of things that make you happy.

Make a class chart of everyone's 'happy face'.

Write a five-line poem using the letters of the word 'happy' to start each line.

List all the films and/or videos that have made you feel happy.

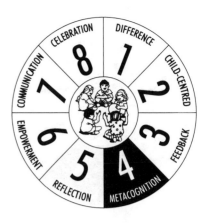

2 COMPREHENSION

Draw a cartoon strip showing something that happened to you that made you happy.

Choose six books and predict whether their endings will be happy or sad.

Referring to Remy Charlip's (1969 or 1964) book *What Good Luck, What Bad Luck*, ascertain how many times the character was happy.

Make a play or a mime about something that makes you happy.

3 APPLICATION

Cut out some articles from newspapers and paste them under the headings 'Happy' and 'Sad'.

Design and construct a machine that makes people happy.

💡 Read a joke or riddle book and choose the five funniest jokes or riddles to share.

💡 Write down all the colours you can think of, then classify them under the headings 'Happy colours' and 'Sad colours'.

4 ANALYSIS

💡 Design a questionnaire to survey what makes people happy.

💡 Organise and plan a 'happy' day for your class or school.

💡 Examine what makes you happy and compare it with what makes other people happy.

💡 Write a TV commercial to sell the product 'Happy'.

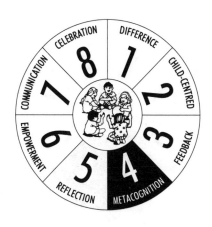

5 SYNTHESIS

💡 Choose your favourite pop CD (compact disc) and design a cover jacket for it.

💡 Write lyrics for a happy song using a familiar melody.

💡 Create a new product that will make people happy.

💡 Imagine you can make three people happy: who would you choose, and why?

6 EVALUATION

Judge whether or not it is good to be happy all the time.

Make a booklet about rules for happiness.

How would you handle people who like to be sad?

Write a letter to the prime minister suggesting changes that would make people happy.

• TEACHING STRATEGIES

CONTRACTS OR PROJECTS
Contracts or projects can be organised on an individual, group or class basis – whichever suits your teaching style.

A whole-class contract could involve organising a 'happy' day. The class could decide to allocate various tasks to particular groups, or an individual child could undertake to make a booklet about rules for happiness.

LEARNING CENTRES

According to Charles (1980), learning centres could be set up for children to work on displayed challenges from each level of Bloom's *Taxonomy*.

A DAILY CHALLENGE

Setting a daily challenge is a good way to stimulate children's interest in a particular topic. Use an activity or question from any level of Bloom's *Taxonomy* in order to challenge groups or the whole class. It is important to plan for a 'sharing' time during which responses can be compared.

One day's challenge could be to find the funniest riddle or joke.

5 REFLECTION

Provision of opportunities for reflection

GUIDEPOSTS

PREREQUISITE UNDERSTANDINGS AND BELIEFS

As a teacher, do you
• believe that reflection is an important part of the learning process?
• make time for your own reflection?
• plan times for children to reflect on their learning?

EFFECTIVE STRATEGIES FOR CLASSROOM IMPLEMENTATION

○ Make provision for reflection in your program.

○ Teach children reflection skills.

○ Vary the methods of reflection – thinking, talking, writing – on an individual, group and whole-class basis.

○ Model the reflection process.

○ Encourage metacognition and, when appropriate, relevant action.

It was morning 'sharing' time in Maryanne's Year 3–4 class. Next to her chair, Maryanne was unwinding what looked like a large roller-blind on a frame.

'Okay, who would like to put today's date on our "reflection" roll?' asked Maryanne. One of the children wrote the day and date using colourful felt pens.

'Is it a special day for anyone?' asked Maryanne.

'Yes, it's my birthday today,' said Mia.

'And my pet hamster had three babies,' offered Brad.

'Okay; some time today, could you record these special events on our roll?' invited Maryanne.

During the day, other pieces of information that the children believed were important were added to the roll, such as

*   'James learnt to skip today,' and
*   'Nicki wrote a fantastic story about a haunted house.'

As each day finished, the roll was wound on to a fresh piece of paper. At the end of the week (or every two weeks), the roll was laid out on the floor and the children were able to walk around it, reflecting on shared experiences and happenings.

Once a term, the roll was unwound along a corridor and parents were invited to share in the experience of reflecting on a term's events.

Maryanne was constantly amazed at the details of the events that all the children were able to recall and reflect on after hearing only a few words about them or after seeing a representative drawing card or symbol attached to a particular 'day'.

One of her responsibilities as a teacher was to ensure that every child made some contribution to the 'reflection' roll, and she herself would often add some of her own achievements and experiences, such as 'Miss Winthorp won her squash game last night.'

The 'reflection' roll encouraged the children to reflect as a whole class and, at the same time, to build a common bond through participating in events and daily happenings.

IDEAS FOR EFFECTIVE STRATEGIES

 Use Kagan's (1990) 'think–pair–share' strategy.

 VISUALISATION

Visualisation is a process through which a person is enabled to create images of an object, a situation or an event in his or her mind. By using this approach, teachers support children by reflecting on their learning.

It is important that children are seated comfortably, and they may wish to close their eyes while the reflective visualisation takes place.

A teacher may organise a short reflective visualisation session such as the following.

> 'Make sure you are sitting comfortably, and close your eyes if you wish. I will ask you to remember some things, and I would like you to make pictures of them inside your head. I may ask you some questions, and I would like you to answer them inside your head as well. Think back to our maths session this morning. Make a picture inside your head about yourself working at one thing from your maths contract. Did you do the activity well? Did you enjoy it? Was there anything you found difficult about it? Who did you work with? Did you work well with that person?
>
> Imagine yourself moving to another activity from your contract sheet. Make a picture of you beginning that activity.
>
> Did you begin well? Did you enjoy the activity? Was there anything difficult about what you did? Did you complete the activity?
>
> Now I'll count to ten, and I want you to open your eyes slowly and come back together as a group: one, two, three ...

In any visualisation process it is important that the teacher slowly ask the questions and make the statements in a quiet voice, giving the children ample time to create the required images.

Some children may wish to share their visualisations; others may not, and teachers have to follow up any visualisation session with sensitivity.

 **TEACHER'S LEARNING LOG**
The teacher models reflection by sharing his or her learning log or reflection journal, a sample entry of which follows.

I went to squash last night and I played a terrible game.
I just didn't seem to be able to hit the ball, and when I did
hit it, it went the wrong way. I got beaten in three straight sets.
There are three other people in my team and they were just great.
They didn't get angry because I lost; they just said not to worry about
it and that I'd be back to my old form next week. That made me
feel lots better. They even took me out for a coffee and cake
after the game to cheer me up!

You must have
nice friends!

I think you will play good again.

It was nice of them to cheer you up.

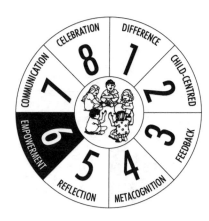

6 EMPOWERMENT

Empowerment of children as learners

GUIDEPOSTS

> **PREREQUISITE UNDERSTANDINGS AND BELIEFS**

As a teacher, do you
- believe that children can be responsible for their own learning?
- acknowledge the effectiveness of peer learning?
- acknowledge your role as a facilitator in the learning process?
- design developmentally appropriate learning experiences?

> **EFFECTIVE STRATEGIES FOR CLASSROOM IMPLEMENTATION**

- Include opportunities for making choices throughout your program.

- Provide appropriate learning opportunities so realistic expectations can be achieved. ('Build in' success.)

- Plan and design for co-operative-learning opportunities.

- Teach skills of problem solving and co-operation.

- Provide appropriate resources and organise children's access to them.

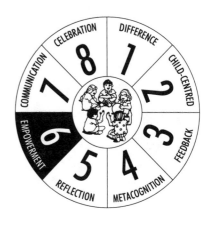

THE PATHWAY IN PRACTICE: A VIGNETTE

Chris's Year 4 class members were very excited after going on an excursion to the beach, where they collected lots of natural items such as shells, seaweed and rocks.

They were sitting in a circle and had many of their treasures in front of them in ice-cream containers, buckets and so on.

'Okay, we seem to have collected some marvellous specimens,' said Chris. What do you think we ought to do with them?'

'I want to make something with my shells –' said Anna, 'one of those shell "animals" like I've seen in the gift shop.'

'Okay,' said Chris, 'who would like to work with Anna? I think we might have to look for some 'Aquadhere' glue in the art area so the shells will stick.'

Several children indicated they would like to make shell 'animals'.

'I want to classify my seaweed into different types,' said Ben. 'I know where there's a book that shows you the names of all the different varieties.'

'Who would like to work on this with Ben?' asked Chris, and several children indicated they would like to do that.

'How will you be able to show us the different sorts of seaweed, Ben?' asked Chris.

'I'm going to get a shirt box from the box-storage area and display each one with its name and information underneath.'

'Sounds great,' said Chris. 'Maria, what are you going to do with those interesting pieces of driftwood you collected?'

'Well, I'm not sure,' said Maria. 'I really like them but I need some ideas on how to use them.'

'I know –' said Kelly, 'we could use them to make a wall hanging. Remember last term when Mia's mum came in and showed us how to do macrame? There's heaps of wool left over in the art area; we could use that.'

The discussion continued until all the students had negotiated what they would do and how they would use the materials they had collected. They had also chosen whether to work by themselves, with a partner or with a group.

IDEAS FOR EFFECTIVE STRATEGIES

Make sure all resources are labelled and have specific locations.

Use curriculum-based contracts and/or integrated contracts.

Encourage the use of learning logs.

Include times for reflection for individuals, groups and the whole class.

Encourage the writing of individual learning proposals.

PROPOSAL WRITING

According to Waters' and Montgomery's *Children Writing Proposals*, proposal writing is about children making written contracts or statements about what they intend to learn.

Having proposals helps children focus on particular areas of interest, thereby empowering them to take responsibility for their own learning.

Proposals can be used by any age group – a teacher or an older child can 'scribe' for young children – and can cover any curriculum area.

It is important that teachers support children's proposal writing by making sure that appropriate resources are available and that adequate time is set aside for group sharing when the proposals are completed.

Following are two proposal-writing vignettes.

VIGNETTE 1: SKIPPING

Lorne's class members were concentrating on improving their skipping as part of a focus on development of gross motor skills. Heath's proposal looked like the one on this page.

> 20th Feb.
>
> I didn't used to like skipping, but now I do I can do criss-cross and double rope and next I'm going to do double dutch.

VIGNETTE 2: BUTTERFLIES
Sue's class members were studying butterflies as a result of a visit to a local butterfly farm. Through negotiation techniques such as brainstorming, Sue established what the children already knew about butterflies, then, as a group, what else they wished to find out. From this process, many children – and Sue – elected to write their own individual proposals. Sue's own proposal looked like the one on this page.

16th July

I have always wondered where butterflies went when it rains so I am going to see if I can find out the answer to this question.

Also, I wonder how many different types of butterflies there are throughout the world?

I hope to have the answers to these questions by next Tuesday.

Sue Graham

7 COMMUNICATION

Acknowledgement of the critical nature of
quality communication

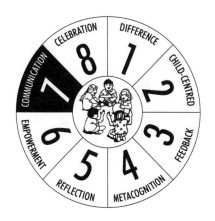

GUIDEPOSTS

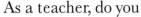

PREREQUISITE UNDERSTANDINGS AND BELIEFS

As a teacher, do you
- communicate in order to achieve shared understandings?
- acknowledge the importance of non-verbal language?
- use positive language?
- try to influence rather than control?
- believe that effective communication is very much a two-way process?
- accept differences in children's ways of communicating?

EFFECTIVE STRATEGIES FOR CLASSROOM IMPLEMENTATION

○ Model effective communication strategies.

○ Plan to ensure that effective communication is integral to your program.

○ Ensure that verbal and non-verbal communication are consistent with each other.

○ Respond to negative situations by using positive language.

○ Use communication methods that are explicit and situation-specific.

○ Respect any situation-specific confidentialities.

○ Practise active listening both with yourself and other people.

THE PATHWAY IN PRACTICE: A VIGNETTE

Vicki was having 'tidying up' time with the twenty-three members of her pre-school morning group. She walked from group to group, asking children to tidy up and come to the mat.

'I want to leave my building up,' said Tim, who had been using the 'Lego'.

'Well, what do we do, then?' asked Vicki.

Tim remembered the agreed procedure and went off to find a piece of paper on which he would put his name for labelling his building. This would communicate to other class members that Tim's building was to be left and not packed away.

After the class had sat on the mat for a short 'sharing' time about the local show, Vicki indicated to the children individually that they may wash their hands and collect their morning playlunch. She did this by holding up a large card that had each child's name printed clearly on it. Children moved quietly to get their food, one at a time.

During playlunch time, Margaret approached Vicki, saying, 'Andrew says he doesn't want me to sit next to him.'

'What do you think you should do about this?' asked Vicki quietly.

'Come and tell you,' responded Margaret.

'And what do you think I will say?' asked Vicki gently.

'I think you'll say that I need to think what to do,' said Margaret.

'All right,' said Vicki, 'have a think, and then decide what you would like to do.'

Margaret paused for a few seconds, then walked over to Andrew. 'You made me feel really sad when you said I couldn't sit next to you, and I really would like to.'

'I'm sorry,' said Andrew. 'You can sit here – do you want a bit of my mandarin?'

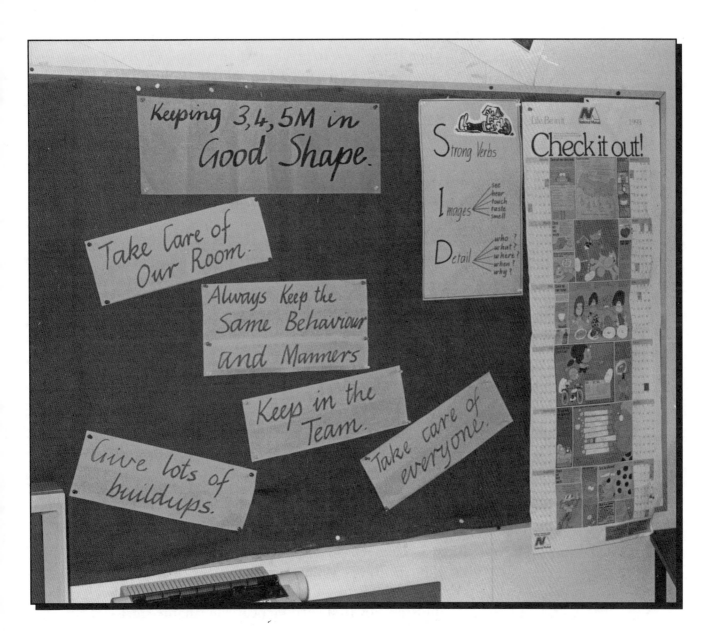

 IDEAS FOR EFFECTIVE STRATEGIES

CLASS MEETINGS

Following is Glasser's (1969) suggested format for class meetings. Teachers will find that some aspects have to be adapted to meet the needs of particular groups of children.

Before embarking on class meetings, teachers and children should

- be aware of the range of topics that can be brought to them,
- realise that once you have made the commitment to hold them they have to be held whenever necessary,
- acknowledge the need for confidentiality: what is said in the meeting stays in the meeting, and
- negotiate and accept the rules before introducing the meeting format.

• SUGGESTED FORMAT

1 The children sit on the floor in a circle. Place an object, such as a basket or small potplant, in the middle of the circle. This gives everyone a central focus and maintains the circle formation if individual children have to move during the session.

2 Give each child his or her own name card and place it on the floor in front of him or her.

3 Declare the meeting open and appoint a 'scribe'. (For younger children, a tape recorder or an older child can fill this role.)

4 As a group, read out the rules for class meetings and clarify any rules if necessary.

5 Ask 'Who has a problem he or she would like the meeting to address?' Request that the children who have a problem indicate their response by turning over their name cards.

6 Ask one of these children to describe his or her problem to the meeting. When the problem has been described, indicate to the children that they may ask clarifying questions by first turning over their name cards.

7 Use the next section of the meeting for class members to suggest possible solutions to the problem presented.

8 Accept and record all solutions, then read them back – or play them back on tape – to the person who has the problem.

9 After the child who presented the problem has listened carefully, invite her to choose two solutions that she would like to put into operation and to tell the meeting which options she has chosen.

10 If time allows, address either a second problem from another child or a class problem, using the same process.

11 Thank everyone for their participation and close the meeting.

 'LISTENING' DAYS: A VIGNETTE

Jackie, a very talented early-childhood teacher, found this very successful method of encouraging her class members to listen.

At the beginning of the year, everyone made headbands that had large 'ears' attached to them. The children decorated them and were able to identify their own 'ears' very easily.

When it was time for the children to listen to Jackie or to each other, they 'put their ears on'.

Using this very simple but highly effective strategy we are teaching young children about appropriate times for listening and are thereby contributing to the instigation of quality communication.

 'SECRET MESSAGES'

Hancock and Blaby (1989) suggest sitting children in a circle and whispering to one child a short message to pass to the person sitting on his or her right. The message is whispered from person to person until it comes back to the original sender. The message received by the original sender is compared with the original message, and reflection takes place about why the message became changed – if that was the case – and how important listening skills are.

 GIVING DIRECTIONS: THE 'ROBOT' GAME

Walker (1983) suggests choosing one child to be the 'robot' who leaves the room. The other class members decide where to place a small object such as a block or small toy. The 'robot' re-enters the room, and the group members take turns at giving him one direction at a time in order to get him to where he can see the object.

The rules of the game are as follows.

- Use only commands such as 'Left!', 'Right!', 'Backwards!', 'Forwards!', 'Stop!' and 'Turn!'
- Do not use names of people or pieces of furniture.
- The 'robot' must do exactly what each director commands.
- As soon as the 'robot' can see the object, he states, in a 'robotic' voice, 'I have the object in my viewfinder,' and another child takes a turn at being the 'robot'.

'AUTHOR'S CIRCLE'

Following writing sessions, the whole class or groups of children sit in a circle in order to share their written work.

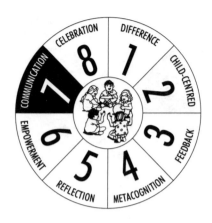

 'CONSTRUCTIVE CONTROVERSY'

The following idea for a 'constructive controversy' is adapted from Dalton's (1992) workshop strategy 'The True Story of the Three Little Pigs' (from Jon Scieszka's book of the same name).

Before commencing the strategy, it is essential to have whole-class or group discussion about the following two rules.

1　Everyone is entitled to his or her own opinion, and this has to be respected.

2　You can disagree with someone's ideas without putting the person down.

• SUGGESTED FORMAT

1　Read the story and share it with the whole class.

2　Use a random grouping process so that the children form groups of four. Ask the children in each group to be 'A', 'B', 'C' or 'D':

A	B
C	D

3　Get 'A' and 'B' to talk together in order to take the side of the three little pigs, and 'C' and 'D' to talk together to take the wolf's side.

4　Get the group to join together and each pair to present its case and shares its perspectives:

A	B Pigs' perspective
C	D Wolf's perspective

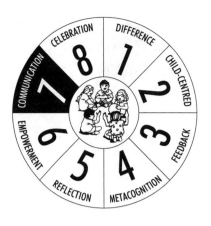

5 After both sides have presented their perspectives, ask the pairs to reverse their positions:

A	B Wolf's perspective
C	D Pigs' perspective

6 Ask each group of four to come up with one statement about the story which everyone in the group agrees on.

7 Share the statements with the whole class.

Reflection is clearly a major component of this activity – asking children to share their feelings and how they felt at different stages of the process.

A 'constructive controversy' not only encourages children's communication skills; it provides them with an opportunity to consider issues from different perspectives.

It is important that the content be fun in order to enable the children to focus on the skills and processes they are using.

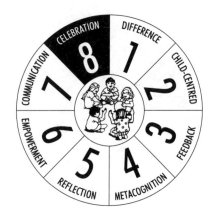

8 CELEBRATION

Acknowledgement of the importance of celebration in the learning process

GUIDEPOSTS

PREREQUISITE UNDERSTANDINGS AND BELIEFS

As a teacher, do you
- believe that celebration is part of the learning process?
- recognise and value the importance of celebration?
- celebrate your own learning?
- negotiate with children ways to celebrate?
- believe in including parents and the whole school community in celebrating children's learning?

EFFECTIVE STRATEGIES FOR CLASSROOM IMPLEMENTATION

○ Ensure that time for celebration is allocated throughout your planning.

○ Create opportunities to celebrate as a class, as groups and as individuals.

○ Plan for celebration within the classroom, within the school and within the community.

○ Model that celebration is about the individual and shared learning, not about external rewards: we learn to walk and talk, for example, without receiving stamps, stickers and so on.

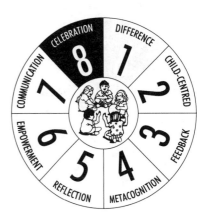

THE PATHWAY IN PRACTICE: A VIGNETTE

Our experiences of schooling may not always be positive. For some groups of children, a couple of years of stereotyping – both in and out of school – can mean they come to reflect the stereotyping by making comments such as, 'We're no good; we're the worst class in the school,' and, 'They can't read; they're stupid.'

Lorne was faced with a situation that included some of these negative perceptions, but she brought to the class personal and professional convictions that provided the bases for transformations. Her convictions are about each child's uniqueness and capacity to learn. She translated her convictions into classroom strategies in order to build children's self-worth so that they began to believe in themselves as learners and feel they had achieved something from their learning.

Children and teacher now celebrate their learning in actions such as hugging, singing, sharing in circles in class, and mounting quality displays of the material outcomes of learning. In the beginning, however, the pervasive obstacles of lack of co-operation and communication skills had prevented them from learning effectively. Through Lorne's consistent caring, modelling and quiet insistence on appropriate be-haviours, the children are progressively acquiring the all-important skills of communication and co-operation.

One way they celebrated their achievements was by holding a 'lolly' day. In the same way as everyone had contributed to their class's learning successes, everyone – individually and collectively – enjoyed the lolly-day celebration. The lolly day was an impromptu response to the children's achievements, not a pre-announced 'bribe', and it modelled the teacher's belief in, and preference for, encouraging the valuing of intrinsic rather than extrinsic rewards. The significance of the lolly day is that the children were not working in order to get a lolly day as such: when they began, neither the children nor the teacher had specific notions of how they would celebrate their progress.

It is important that celebration be 'part and parcel' of the whole, continuous process of learning, not an 'end' attach-ment. Little celebrations along the way provide acknowledge-ment, as do the usual culminations involving presentations and displays.

IDEAS FOR EFFECTIVE STRATEGIES

Effectively display children's work in local shops, businesses and so on.

Plan whole-class 'celebration' days. Teachers and children can brainstorm and negotiate these. Some ideas for 'celebrating' are as follows.
- A concert
- A picnic
- An 'expo' day
- A barbecue
- A 'thank you' day
- A corroboree

 ### 'AFFIRMATION' GAMES

• 'MAGIC CIRCLE'
See the 'Difference' pathway on page 7.

• THE 'HUMAN-TREASURE HUNT'
N. and T. Graves (1990) suggest children and teacher be given a list of positive attributes to find within the group, then writing one person's name next to each phrase. A list could look like the one on page 61.

Find someone who . . .

* is a great listener.   Jo

* laughs a lot.   Anna

* shares cheerfully.   Tania

* is a good team member.

* enjoys helping other people.

* tries his or her best.

Because one of this activity's purposes is to build positive interactions, it is important that adequate time be allowed to achieve this.

Following the activity, use 'reflective questioning' in order to maximise the positive outcomes for everyone involved. Some 'reflective questions' are as follows.

- 'What did you find easy about this task?'
- 'What was something new you discovered about yourself or someone else?'
- 'Where else could you find a "human-treasure hunt"?'
- 'What was the most interesting thing you discovered?'
- 'What other questions could we have asked?'

💡 Invite parents to 'We can' or 'Look at what we've done' mornings.

💡 **RAPS**

Using raps is an approach that is multi-sensory, and this can accelerate learning in a fun way by tapping into our sense of rhythm and movement.

Raps are an ideal way of celebrating success and building class culture.

VIGNETTE: 'LORNE'S CLASS RAP'
Lorne's class composed the rap that appears on the class noticeboard in the photograph on this page.

GROUP CELEBRATION OF CO-OPERATION

• THE 'LAP SIT'

N. and T. Graves (1990) suggest standing all the class members very closely together in a circle, all children facing the same direction, one child behind the other. On the count of three, each individual child sits gently on the lap of the person directly behind her. Having a photograph or video of the event is a good way to preserve this moment of co-operative celebration.

PART TWO

Integration of the pathways for transference of learning

Using incorporated examples, Part Two shows how various pathways may be integrated within individual lessons or units of work. When planning is approached in this way, the outcome is co-operative learning through which children are challenged and their basic needs can be fulfilled. By using the pathways as a framework, teachers ensure that they are providing for success-oriented classrooms in which children and teachers form a community of learners.

The three sections of Part Two are as follows.

1 A co-operative language experience
2 Planning and setting up a learning centre
3 A co-operative science unit

1 A CO-OPERATIVE LANGUAGE EXPERIENCE

This structure can be used with a variety of books or stories. By adjusting the group tasks, the process can be used with Prep to Year 5 classes. For this particular lesson we have used Sue Lock's book *Hubert Hunts his Hum*, and the following lesson has been developed for children in Year 1, 2 or 3.

COMMUNICATION

1   Read, share and discuss the book with the whole class, ensuring that the children have an understanding of words such as 'accountant' and 'subway'.

2   Randomly group your class into five groups and choose a 'scribe'. In order to avoid argument, a good strategy is to ask 'the person wearing green' or 'the person who has the longest hair' to be the 'scribe' for each group.

EMPOWERMENT

3   Give each group a large sheet of butcher's paper and a felt pen. At the top of each sheet, write a question that offers alternatives to the text. For example,
    • 'Where else might Harry have lived?'
    • 'What other job could Harry have had?'
    • 'Where else could Harry have looked inside?'
    • 'Where else could Harry have looked outside?'
    • 'Had Harry not found his whistle, what other noise might he have made?'

DIFFERENCE

4   Get the children to brainstorm in groups and the 'scribe' to write and accept *all* responses.

5   When groups have a number of ideas, ask them to go into a 'head huddle'. Only thirty seconds is allowed for this, and the group members have to agree on one response they would like to share. The 'scribe' circles this response.

6   Bring the class back together and create a new text using each group's chosen response. This can be done by the teacher on butcher's paper or on an overhead transparency.

7   It may be necessary, as a group, to edit this text in order to accommodate class responses.

Harry Hunts his Whistle

'Harry was a man who lived in a _____.

He was a _____.

One day he lost his whistle and he was so sad.

He looked everywhere inside – even _____.

He looked everywhere outside – even _____,
but he just couldn't find his whistle.

Just when he was about to give up, he found out he could _____.

He was so happy, he didn't miss his whistle after all.'

8 Ask the children to reflect on how their responses have changed the story. Give the groups and the class some feedback on how they worked together on the activity.

FEEDBACK

Some suggestions for the many options that individuals or groups might wish to extend are as follows.

REFLECTION

Illustrate the new text.

Use the children's 'brainstorming' sheets in order for them to make up their own story or stories.

CHILD-CENTRED

Decide on other aspects of the story which they could change.

Plan a celebration for Harry having found his alternative sound.

Display and share with other classes.

2 PLANNING AND SETTING UP A LEARNING CENTRE

Learning centres are very effective ways of encouraging children to work *independently* and *interdependently*. The centres can cater for different learning styles and are a flexible and motivating strategy.

It is very important that the materials necessary for putting a learning centre together be prepared and readily at hand. Some materials you may find useful are as follows.

- Corrugated cardboard
- Bricks
- Small tables
- Hessian-covered or painted boxes
- Baskets
- Laminated cards
- Bookstands

See the photographs on pages 72 and 73.

Learning centres can be used in many ways.

CHILD-CENTRED

1 To supplement the class program; for example, a child may bring in some object that captures the class's or a group's interest, and the object can then provide a focus for the learning centre

2 As an integral part of the program

3 As the total basis for organising the program

Learning centres can be used by the following groups.

DIFFERENCE

1 A whole class

2 A particular group of children who

EMPOWERMENT

- have a special interest,
- require particular skills development,
- are able to demonstrate a reasonable amount of independence, or
- require extension and enrichment

3 Different groups of children within a class at different times

Learning centres can include the following.

1 Something every child can complete

2 Activities that provide challenges for every child

3 Individual and small-group activities

4 Activities that require children to use resources

5 Activities that cater for and develop social interests

6 Activities that encourage a variety of learning modes, for example using our senses, presenting in different ways, observing, experimenting, reading, writing, making and doing

7 Activities that encourage many ways of thinking

Bloom's *Taxonomy* provides a good model that helps in meeting a range of abilities, interests and requirements.

Routines, procedures and expectations for using learning centres have to be well established with the children before introducing them into your program.

Routines and explanation of learning challenges have to be made clear on a daily basis. Following are five examples.

1 Establish how many people may use the learning centre at one time.

2 Establish the times they may be used.

3 Select activities: are some compulsory and others optional?

4 Once an activity is chosen it should be understood it will be completed.

5 Some children may require guiding to certain activities in order to ensure that their requirements are met and that they are being challenged.

Learning centres can be evaluated by using any of the following four methods.

1 Observing children using the centre

2 Having sign-in charts

3 Using learning logs

4 Having a comment book for the children to write in

METACOGNITION
AND DIFFERENCE

FEEDBACK

EXAMPLE: A MATHS LEARNING CENTRE

Focus: Nature numbers

Purpose: To focus the children on investigation of number in the environment

Who: All the children from the class to work at the learning centre as part of their daily contract

When: At predetermined times during the day, six children at a time will be working at the centre

CELEBRATION

EVALUATION (*Communication*)
The children 'sign in' to the learning centre on a class list. At the end of each day there is class sharing on the activities tried.

Use the following table as a suggestion for setting out the learning challenges.

Number of learning challenges						
	Today's date is _____.	1	2	3	4	5
John	John	X			/	
Bela						
Sam	Sam		/			
Tom						
Sue	Sue		/		X	
Ara						

[/] Has begun a challenge (*Feedback*)
[X] Has completed a challenge

SETTING UP
Arrange large boxes, tables and so on to hold the resources.

SUGGESTED MATERIALS
Use materials the children have collected, such as seed pods, bark, a variety of leaves, and coconuts. To these, add a set of 'balance' scales, photographs of trees, some seeds, a ruler, a recording chart, and any other resources that may be required.

SOME LEARNING CHALLENGES USING THESE MATERIALS

1 'Estimate how many seeds would have been in this pod.'

2 'Which tree did this bark come from?' (Photographs of trees would accompany this challenge.)

3 'Match these leaves to the rubbings.' 'Make your own rubbings.'

4 'How many small leaves fit on the large leaf? Write your answer in your maths book.'

5 'Find three things that are heavier than this coconut. Draw them.'

6 'Measure which seed travels the furthest when you blow on the seeds. Record your answer on this chart.'

All the materials required for completing the learning challenges should be easily accessible at the learning centre.

Challenges can be changed whenever a teacher believes this is necessary.

All children do not have to complete every challenge.

FEEDBACK

3 A CO-OPERATIVE SCIENCE UNIT

Jeannie Baker's book *Window* has been used in Year 6–7 as a focus in language development. The teacher John Peterson mentions it as a link for explorations into the forces of erosion, as follows.

'We've been talking about changes to the earth that are made by people. During the next few weeks we will explore two ideas: one, the idea of natural forces changing the earth, and two, the idea of people modifying the effects of these natural forces.'

'Do you mean erosion, sir?'

'Yes, Robert, and I'd like us to be thinking about it for our first discussion and planning session next week.'

On the following Tuesday, the whole class brainstormed suggestions for exploring erosion by using the following three headings.

- 'What do we know?'
- 'What do we think we know?'
- 'What do we want to find out?'

John, the teacher, commented, 'We have a good start to our exploring. Let's clarify what we know by doing six experiments. Our jobs will be to observe and record the effects of water on a heap of

- sand,
- clay and
- dirt,

and the effects of wind on a heap of

- sand,
- clay and
- dirt.'

The children got into groups of six, and the 'jigsaw' strategy was used in order for them to conduct the experiments and share the outcomes with their home group.

'Today we've clarified and confirmed what we know about wind and water erosion. To take our exploration further, we have to work on what we think we know and what we have to find out. We'll also have to bring our knowledge and learning together somehow. One way of achieving this is to think of how we could help other people to learn about erosion.'

'How could we do this?' The children's suggestions included

FEEDBACK

CHILD-CENTRED

EMPOWERING

RECOGNITION OF DIFFERENCE

METACOGNITION

CHILD-CENTRED

- making a learning centre,
- making an activity workbook, and
- making up some games about erosion.

'Okay, you have some excellent ideas there,' commended John. 'In pairs or groups of no more than five, decide which one you will use. Work to have your erosion learning project ready in three weeks.'

'Then we'll try them out on each other and invite Mrs Walker's Year 5 (or 6 or 7) from next door to have a go as well.'

FEEDBACK

EMPOWERING

CELEBRATION

REFERENCES

Baker, J. 1991, *Window*, Random Century Pty Ltd, Sydney.

Belenky, M. F., McVicker Clinchy, B., Goldberger, N. R. and Tarule, J. M. 1986, *Women's Ways of Knowing*, Basic Books – a Division of Harper Collins Publishers, New York.

Bloom, B. S. (ed.) 1956, *Taxonomy of Educational Objectives, Handbook I: Cognitive Domain*, Longmans, Green and Co. Ltd, London.

Bloom, B. S. (ed.) 1956, *Taxonomy of Educational Objectives, Handbook II: Affective Domain*, Longmans, Green and Co. Ltd, London.

Butler, J. 1992, *From Action to Thought: the Fulfilment of Human Potential*, paper presented at Fifth International Thinking Conference, July 1992, Townsville, Queensland.

Charles, C. M. 1980, *Individualising Instruction*, The C. V. Mosby Company, St Louis, Missouri.

Charlip, R. 1964, 1969, *What Good Luck, What Bad Luck*, Scholastic Book Services – a Division of Scholastic Magazines Inc., by arrangement with Parents Magazine Press, publisher of the 1964 edition under the title *Fortunately*, fifth printing, March 1974, United States.

Collis, M. and Dalton, J. 1989, *Becoming Responsible Learners*, Eleanor Curtain Publishing, Melbourne.

Covey, S. R. 1989, *The Seven Habits of Highly Effective People*, The Business Library, Simon and Schuster, New York.

Dalton, J. 1985, *Adventures in Thinking*, Thomas Nelson Australia, Melbourne.

Dalton, J. 1992, 'Constructive controversy', workshop strategy.

Dwyer, J. 1989, *A Sea of Talk*, Primary English Teaching Association, Sydney.

Fleet, A. and Martin, L. 1985, *Making it Work*, Thomas Nelson Australia, Melbourne.

Gibbs, J. 1987, *Tribes*, Center Source Publications, Santa Rosa, California.

Glasser, W. 1965, 1975, *Reality Therapy: a New Approach to Psychiatry*, Perennial Library edition, Harper and Row Publishers, New York.

Glasser, W. 1969, *Schools Without Failure*, Perennial Library edition, Harper and Row Publishers, New York.

Glasser, W. 1986, *Control Theory in the Classroom*, Perennial Library edition, Harper and Row Publishers, New York.

Graves, N. and Graves, T. 1990, *A Part to Play*, Latitude Publications, Melbourne.

Grundy, S. 1987, *Curriculum: Product or Praxis?*, The Falmer Press, Lewes, East Sussex.

Habermas, J. 1968, *Knowledge and Human Interests*, translated by Jeremy J. Shapiro; copyright 1971, Beacon Press, Boston.

Habermas, J. 1976, *Communication and the Evolution of Society*, translated by Thomas McCarthy; copyright 1979, Beacon Press, Boston.

Habermas, J. 1981, *The Theory of Communicative Action, Volume I: Reason and the Rationalisation of Society*, Suhrkamp Verlag, Frankfurt am Main, translated by Thomas McCarthy; copyright 1984, Beacon Press, Boston.

Hancock, K. and Blaby, B. 1989, *People Interacting*, Thomas Nelson Australia, Melbourne.

Hill, S. 1992, *Games that Work*, Eleanor Curtain Publishing, Melbourne.

Hill, S. and Hill, T. 1990, *The Collaborative Classroom*, Eleanor Curtain Publishing, Melbourne.

Kagan, S. 1990. *Think–Pair–Share*, cited Hill 1992, page 6.

Lock, S. 1980, *Hubert Hunts his Hum*, a 'Read it Again' book, Ashton Scholastic, by arrangement with Puffin Books.

McVitty, W. (ed.) 1986, *Getting it Together*, Bridge Printery Pty Ltd, Sydney.

Samples, B. 1987, *Open Mind Whole Mind: Parenting and Teaching Tomorrow's Children Today*, Jalmar Press, California.

Scieszka, J. 1989, *The True Story of the Three Little Pigs*, Puffin Books, published by the Penguin Group, Penguin Books Australia Ltd, Melbourne.

Tasmanian Department of Education, Curriculum Branch. 1989, 'Primary Focus' video, Program 7: a video 'magazine' of news and developments in primary schools.

Turner, A. (ed.) 1992, *Patterns of Thinking*, Primary English Teaching Association, Sydney.

Walker, D. 1983, 'Giving directions', strategy in practice.

Walker, D. and Brown, P. 1992, 'Child-centred cycle', strategy in practice.

Walker, D. and Ferencz, L. 1982, strategy in practice.

Waters, M. and Montgomery, P. 1992, *Children Writing Proposals: Clarifying What they Know and What they Want to Find Out*, in *Reading Around* 1991–92 series, P. Smith (ed.), Australian Reading Association Ltd.

INDEX OF GAMES AND ACTIVITIES

BOOKS FOR CO-OPERATIVE LEARNING FROM ELEANOR CURTAIN PUBLISHING

Together is Better
Collaborative assessment, evaluation and reporting
Anne Davies, Caren Cameron, Colleen Politano, Kathleen Gregory

Together is Better shows how teachers, students and parents can work together to evaluate children's learning in a three-way process. The book provides many valuable examples of and strategies for collaboration:
* the process of three-way reporting
* the process of three-way conferencing
* setting learning goals and evaluation criteria with students and parents
* helping students to recognise and evaluate their own learning
* informal reports and other communication techniques
* guidelines and inventories for complete reports

All strategies and guidelines are fully supported with practical activities and examples of documentation needed. This large-format, highly illustrated book is inviting to use. Written for classroom teachers, administrators, and pre-service teachers, it will give all readers the confidence to try new approaches to evaluation.

ISBN 1 875327 19 3 illustrated 140pp

The Collaborative Classroom
A guide to co-operative learning
Susan and Tim Hill

The Collaborative Classroom is a creative and practical guide which focuses on and identifies the areas where co-operative skills are needed: forming groups – working as a group, problem solving as a group; and managing differences – discussing problems, offering suggestions and providing practical applications. *The Collaborative Classroom* includes dozens of activities to get the beginning teacher started.

ISBN 1 875327 00 2 illustrated 162pp

Becoming Responsible Learners
Strategies for positive classroom management
Joan Dalton and Mark Collis

An extremely practical and highly readable book on strategies and guidelines for classroom management, *Becoming Responsible Learners* is the result of observing effective collaborative teachers at work and talking to them about their beliefs and classroom practices. It is an invaluable asset to teachers who want to encourage children to take responsibility for their own learning and behaviour.

ISBN 1 875327 05 3 illustrated 80pp

Raps & Rhymes
Selected by Susan Hill

Raps & Rhymes is a stimulating selection of traditional chants and rhymes that have been played with, improvised on and read by children of all ages. Reading aloud as a group, joining in a chant or a rhyme is a great warm-up to any lesson, and an effective way to build up a feeling of cohesiveness in class.

There are selections for Improvising, Clapping and Clicking, Action Rhymes, Part-reading and just plain Nonsense.

ISBN 1 875327 03 7 illustrated 80pp

Jump for Joy

More raps & rhymes

Susan Hill

Jump for Joy is the exciting successor to Susan Hill's *Raps & Rhymes*, which is so popular in classrooms throughout Australia and has become an instant hit with teachers and children in the USA, Canada and New Zealand. *Jump for Joy* provides a variety of chants and poems for reading aloud, selected with an eye to fun as well as learning. Contents:

* Claps and Clicks
* Games and Actions
* Chants with Two Parts
* Chants with More Voices
* Absolute Nonsense

ISBN   1   875327   17   7   illustrated   64pp

Readers Theatre

Performing the text

Susan Hill

Readers Theatre is a simple, informal and motivating way to involve students in the study of literature by group story-telling, shared reading, improvisation and performance of a favourite story. *Readers Theatre* provides complete scripts for performance, guidelines for helping children write their own scripts, aids and ideas for improvisation and lists of texts that work well in adaptation.

ISBN   1   875327   01   0   illustrated   88pp

Games That Work

Co-operative games and activities for the primary school classroom

Susan Hill

This practical resource presents games and activities to engage children, and to introduce them to the idea and the practice of collaboration. *Games That Work* focuses on communication and co-operation, the underpinning of all learning. The features of collaboration are made explicit and the games are presented not as isolated activities, but as preparation and structuring for group work.

ISBN   1   875327   16   9   illustrated   128pp

For information on these and other titles contact
Eleanor Curtain Publishing
906 Malvern Road, Armadale Australia 3143
Tel. (03) 822 0344 Fax (03) 824 8851

Distributed in New Zealand by
Ashton Scholastic
165 Marua Road, Panmure Auckland
Tel. (09) 579 6089 Fax (03) 579 3860